Love Beyond Measure

A SPIRITUALITY OF NONVIOLENCE

Mary Lou Kownacki, OSB

INTRODUCTION

The writings of Mary Lou Kownacki, OSB, on the spirituality of nonviolence have touched many hearts, but when her essay entitled "The Doorway to Peace" was published in the twentieth anniversary issue of the Pax Christi magazine, the response was overwhelming. Many readers felt that it was the fullest and most powerful expression of her insight into gospel nonviolence. They asked for a stand-alone publication of the essay so it could reach a wider audience. This book is the response to that request.

The core of *Love Beyond Measure* is an unabridged version of Mary Lou's inspiring essay in a format that helps the reader to reflectively and prayerfully digest its insights and challenges. The essay is printed in its entirety at the beginning for those who wish to read it straight through before starting the process. Following the essay is the framework for five sessions, each with a prayer ritual, briefer related readings, and questions for individual reflection or group sharing. Each session focuses on one part of the essay.

The book is intended to be flexible, equally suited to the individual reader or a group process. Obviously the individual reader needs no guidance on pace or procedure. The following suggestions for group participants may be modified or ignored as the group's needs dictate.

It is assumed that each session would be between sixty and ninety minutes long. It would be helpful if participants read at least the main selection (the designated part of Mary Lou Kownacki's essay) before coming together. Whoever is acting as facilitator for the session can divide parts of the opening prayer ritual among the participants. Have a Peace Candle (any large candle) displayed prominently so it can be lighted during the opening song and remain lit during each session.

A typical session begins with a prayer ritual that sets the tone for the session. This is followed by discussion questions about the main reading on which the participants have already reflected. After this, there are several related readings with discussion questions. There are also questions for the scripture used in the prayer ritual. Each session closes with a brief prayer.

The facilitator's role requires no special expertise or extra preparation. But the facilitator needs to act as the informal time manager to move the group to the next question or guide the participants back to the focus if they stray too far afield. It is important that the group have the chance to consider all the readings provided. The selections could be read silently or aloud as the group prefers.

The unity of this whole process derives from the single essay that begins the book and is progressively explored as the primary reading in the sessions. The final session reinforces this unified dynamic by returning to look at the essay as a whole. The importance of this final phase should not be underestimated. Without this step, the fragments of Mary Lou's message may not be sufficiently integrated into the mind and life of the individual readers.

Jim Dinn

LOVE BEYOND MEASURE
A Spirituality of Nonviolence

Essay

PART 1:

DEPTH OF GOD'S LOVE

Nonviolence has a bad reputation. Too many identify it with the snake in the following story: It seems that in a certain village a snake had bitten so many people that few dared to go into the fields. Finally it was taken to a wise person who tamed the snake and persuaded it to practice the discipline of nonviolence.

When the villagers discovered that the snake was harmless, they took to hurling stones at it and dragging it by its tail. Finally the badly battered and disillusioned snake crawled to the wise one and complained bitterly.

"You've stopped frightening people," the wise one said, "and that's bad."

The snake was incredulous. "But it was you who taught me to practice the discipline of nonviolence," the snake replied. "Oh," said the wise one, "I told you to stop hurting people, not stop hissing."

Point: authentic nonviolence does not harm, but it does know when to hiss. It hisses loud and long at every system and structure that trods the weak and powerless underfoot. It hisses so strongly and with such persistence that governments topple and dictatorships dissolve.

When the Filipino people—armed with rosary beads— toppled the Marcos government by kneeling in front of tanks, that was a hiss.

When tens of thousands of students poured into Tiananmen Square bearing this placard: "Although you trod a thousand resisters underfoot, I shall be the one-thousand-and first"—that was a hiss.

The Solidarity movement in Poland with its strikes, slowdowns, boycotts, prison hunger strikes, marches and 500 underground presses calling Poles to nonviolent resistance was a hiss.

So was the massive resistance to the Gorbachev coup attempt and the dismantling of the forced union of Soviet states.

Nonviolence, then, can never be equated with passivity, it is the essence of courage, creativity and action. Nonviolence does, however, require patience: a passionate endurance and commitment to seek justice and truth no matter the cost.

But I am not talking about the history or philosophy or the politics of nonviolence. I do not want to discuss whether nonviolence is more effective than violence in breaking the chains of colonialism and oppression that bind so many of the world's people.

No, I would like to talk about something even more revolutionary, something much more difficult. I would like to address the doorway to peace, a spirituality of nonviolence. Because unless we address that, unless we focus on the underpinning of nonviolent action, any advocacy for nonviolent social change runs the risk of being superficial or worse— hypocritical, masking deep hostility, self-righteousness, and a desire to defeat and humiliate others.

I would like to approach the doorway to peace, then, in the company of an old Hasidic rabbi who each morning crossed the village square on his way to the temple to pray. One morning a large Cossack soldier, who happened to be in a vile mood, accosted him saying, "Hey, Rebby, where are you going?" The old rabbi said, "I don't know." This infuriated the Cossack. "What do you mean you don't know? Every morning for 25 years you've crossed the village square and gone to the temple to pray. Don't fool with me. Who do you think you are, telling me you don't know?"
He grabbed the old rabbi by the coat and dragged him off to jail. Just as he was about to push him into the cell, the rabbi turned to him saying, "You see, I didn't know."

The rabbi models, I think, the proper attitude or approach

to our topic, the spirituality of nonviolence. The rabbi cautions against pretending to know the path that will lead us to a nonviolent heart.

Once upon a time I was sure about nonviolence. I had a clear vision of a nonviolent world and imagined myself walking towards it. But after many years of experimenting with nonviolence, I'm not sure about anything except Ephesians 3: 17-19. In that letter, Paul writes, "May Christ dwell in your hearts through faith, and may charity be the root and foundation of your life. Then may you grasp fully, with all the saints, the breadth and length and height and depth of Christ's love, and experience this love which surpasses all knowledge, so that you may attain to the very fullness of God."

I think a spirituality of nonviolence has something to do with grasping fully the depth and height and length and breadth of Christ's love, experiencing it and making it visible.

Obviously, then, I am undertaking an exercise in frustration. Why? Because Saint Paul reminds us that this way of loving is beyond knowledge, beyond explanation. It is a love that cannot be grasped unless we take a leap in faith while grounding our lives in love.

Therefore, I approach this subject from the kneeling position of Job who, after trying to make sense of God's ways can only testify: "I have spoken of great things which I have not understood, things too wonderful for me to know."

"I HAVE SPOKEN OF GREAT THINGS WHICH I HAVE NOT UNDERSTOOD, THINGS TOO WONDERFUL FOR ME TO KNOW." — JOB

A spirituality of nonviolence has something to do with grasping fully the depth of God's love. When I think of depth, I go inward and down. So a good place to start the journey to nonviolence is by exploring love of self and the depth of God's love for me. Without a true love for oneself, any attempts at nonviolence easily become clanging cymbals and sounding gongs.

After I read my first Gandhi, and marched in my first anti-war demonstration, I steeled myself for a heroic lifestyle of long fasts, solidarity with the poor and civil disobedience. I spent long hours worrying that I wouldn't have the mettle to meet this self-spun scenario. I could have spared myself the agony. Bread and water fasts, rubbing shoulders with the poor, prison cells are easy. A spirituality of nonviolence makes tougher demands. It forces you to stand in front of a mirror and look. And that's not always a pleasant experience.

Gandhi said it well: I have only three enemies. My favorite enemy, the one most easily influenced for the better, is the British nation. My second enemy, the Indian people, is far more difficult. But my most formidable opponent is a man named Mohandas K. Gandhi. With him, I seem to have very little influence."

Obviously, Gandhi is not alone. Every serious student of nonviolence that I've encountered over the years expresses surprise and struggle upon discovering the violence within. They say things like: "I just realized how much I yell at the kids.... I drive through city traffic on a very short fuse.... There is a raging anger in me that explodes when my opinions are questioned.... I just discovered that my enemy is the president, or my boss, or the bishop and I can't tolerate him."

The problem is that once these violent feelings surface, peacemakers tend to panic and beat their breasts, "God, I am not worthy to be a peacemaker." That attitude, however, is not only self-defeating, it is contrary to a spirituality of nonviolence which calls us to go beyond self-knowledge and reach self-acceptance.

They tell about a man who took great pride in his lawn, only to wake up one day and find a large crop of dandelions. He tried every method he knew to get rid of them. Still they

4

plagued him. Finally, he wrote the Department of Agriculture. He enumerated all the things he had tried and closed his letter with the question, "What shall I do now?" In a few weeks the reply came: "We suggest you learn to love them."

To learn to love all the dandelions that live in Mary Lou Kownacki is spiritual maturity. It's only when I can say Yes to myself, as I am, that God can work in me. Otherwise I'm too busy trying to make myself better than God made me. And I get in God's way.

To say Yes to myself might mean that if I accept the weaknesses in myself, I can accept the weaknesses in others more easily. Then there is no need to be so defensive, no need to project my deepest fears about myself on the enemy: US government officials, Saddam Hussein, church hierarchy, leftist radicals, right wing advocates.

The spiritual writer, Henri Nouwen, reminds us that unless we hear and believe the voice that Jesus did, the voice that says: "You are my beloved daughter; you are my beloved son," unless we claim that voice for ourselves our nonviolent actions will be in vain.

Why? Because without a sincere self-love, actions for peace and justice can really be undertaken only to prove to ourselves that we are lovable, that we are worth loving.

Paul Tillich laid out life's greatest challenge: "Simply accept the fact that you are accepted." But we fight it and continue to slap the face of unconditional love.

A spirituality of nonviolence, therefore, has a modest goal: to invite us to self-knowledge and to leap with us to self-acceptance. This is what it means to experience fully the depth of God's love for me. Only then can we take the first step as nonviolent peacemakers.

PART 2

HEIGHT OF GOD'S LOVE

Height moves the eye upward, toward the mountaintop of God's dwelling place. The spiritual writer Anthony DeMello reminded us that we become like the God we adore. If I look back on my life, the God I search for, the God I adore, has passed through many prisms.

My earliest recollections are of a Judge God and this God frightened me. So I kept rituals and worried about rules and eternal fire. Then the novelist Leo Tolstoy introduced me to the God who lived in others, especially the poor and outcast. And I devoted my days to soup kitchens and houses of hospitality.

Then in the Vietnam War days I met the God of the prophets and I confronted the powerful who ground the powerless into dust. Those were the days consumed by picket lines, long fasts, vigils, mass marches and civil disobedience.

Then my heart was snared by the God of peace who is never glorified by human violence. So I went about trying to beat swords into plowshares and spears into pruning hooks.

Lately, I have been searching for and seeking the God of this quotation by Thomas Merton: "I have overshadowed Jonah with my mercy...have you had sight of me, Jonah, my child? Mercy within mercy within mercy." My heart is restless for this God because it is a God I cannot comprehend. Yet I believe that to experience fully the height of God's love I must swim in this ocean of compassion.

So all I do is repeat the mystery and watch carefully. "Have you had sight of me, Mary Lou, my child? Mercy within mercy within mercy." Now and then we catch sight of this unfathomable mercy, now and then we get a glimpse of this compassionate Love.

One of my earliest memories of meeting a compassionate heart took place in the early 60s and it is what attracted me to nonviolence. I can remember being transfixed before the TV as I watched blacks and whites sit at segregated lunch counters. They refused to move until they were served, while angry whites poured ketchup on their heads, smeared mustard through their hair and eyes, and pelted them with racial slurs.

I wondered how people could absorb such hatred and violence without striking back. Then I read an account in the Catholic Worker newspaper where a black man was quoted as saying, "I will let them kick me and kick me until they have kicked all hatred out of themselves and into my own body where I will transform it into love." That unidentified black man is a glimpse of the height of God's love.

Another place where I found it was in hearing the story of Pax Christi's birth. Pax Christi is the international Catholic peace movement.

Pax Christi, Latin for the Peace of Christ, was born in a prison. Not just any prison, but a prison filled with resisters who were waiting to be sent to the concentration camp at Buchenwald. It was World War II and France was occupied by Germany. Herded together in a French state prison were French resistance fighters and others—mainly priests and religious—who had harbored hunted Jews. One of the resistance fighters asked a fellow-prisoner, Bishop Theas, to celebrate Mass. Bishop Theas was in prison for nonviolent resistance—he had condemned, through a pastoral letter, the persecution of Jews, the deportation of French workers to Germany for forced labor, and the reprisal-destruction of whole villages.

The prison was seething with hatred and anger because a few weeks before—in retaliation for the killing of a few Nazi soldiers—the inhabitants of a small village had been herded into the village church and the church set afire. Bishop Theas agreed to celebrate the prison Mass, but he chose for his homily the theme, "Love your enemy." He read to these brave, honorable, courageous French freedom-fighters what they least expected: "Love your enemies, do good to them that hate you, and pray for those that persecute you." Some of the prisoners disrupted the bishop. "This gospel is terrible," they said. "This gospel is impossible to live." Bishop Theas replied, "I cannot preach anything to you but what Jesus said, 'Love your enemies.' Not more—not less."

Then he led the prisoners in the prayer that Jesus taught us. When he came to the line, "Forgive us our trespasses as we forgive those who trespass against us," he paused and added one word—"Germany." We can only imagine the terrible pain and anguish, the shouts and screams ripping through the hearts of the prisoners, "They've killed our children." Certainly, we can understand any explosion of grief and anger. But Bishop Theas gently insisted that this was necessary. He repeated the word—"Germany." Many could not finish the prayer. Some did. All understood, perhaps for the first time, the height of love to which Jesus called us when he taught us how to pray.

Bishop Theas was eventually released from prison, but the incident altered his life. Because of it he was determined to devote the rest of his days to reconciliation efforts between France and Germany. When a French lay woman, Madame Dortel-Claudot, approached him about organizing a prayer crusade for reconciliation between the French and German people, Bishop Theas blessed the effort. This prayer crusade was the beginning of Pax Christi.

Or how about Etty Hillesum, a young Dutch Jewish woman who died in Auschwitz, and whose journals were recently found and published. In a concentration camp, Etty writes an imaginary conversation with a friend: "Yes, life is beautiful and I value it anew at the end of every day, even though I know the sons and daughters of mothers are being murdered in concentration camps. Do not relieve your feelings through hatred, do not seek to be avenged on all German mothers, for they, too, sorrow at this very moment for their slain and murdered children." And in another journal entry, "I believe that I will never be able to hate any human being for their so-called 'wickedness,' that I shall only hate the evil that is within me...."

What does it mean to love like that? What does it mean to bathe creation in such mercy? Certainly the unidentified black man, Pax Christi's birth and Etty Hillesum's journal, offer us an incarnation of the height of God's love.

PART 3

LENGTH OF GOD'S LOVE

To climb the mountain of God's love and reach its peak puts the rest of the world in perspective.

To view salvation history from the merciful heart of God shatters our human definitions of justice and right judgment.

Because our concept of time is so limited we often equate our sense of justice with God's, the success of our actions by daily headlines. But those who experience the length of God's love, measure time and history differently. With the psalmist they pray: "A thousand years in your sight are as yesterday that is past." One struggling to be nonviolent comes to know that God's story is still unfolding and that our lifetime is merely one short phrase in the library of humankind.

With this view of time, how can one despair? And how can one harm another or kill another? Given the vast expanse of God's love affair with humanity, who of us can claim that our truth—no matter how clear it seems today—is the truth. If we wound or kill another, a part of the truth is lost forever and we are the poorer for it.

The point is that we can never know the final outcome of so called good and bad events. For example, all of us rightly rejoiced at the Cold War meltdown in the early 1990's. Certainly, this was an undeniable good. And yet, the 1991 Persian Gulf war became possible only because the Soviet Union no longer held the United States in check. Good event or bad event? Or again, was the Persian Gulf war a completely unredeemable event, or might some good be born from its anguish and labor? Did the Gulf war, for instance, pound the last nail in the coffin of the just war theory, and delegitimize war forever in the church?

Let me offer another example, one closer to my heart, a situation that has tested to the breaking point my faith in nonviolence, my facile words on the length of God's love. My personal journey to nonviolence is closely connected to a country so pathetic, so inconsequential in the eyes of power, so fly-like that even you and I might be tempted to swat it and end its misery. That country is Haiti, a land and people that I have grown to love deeply over the past four years.

The first time I visited this forsaken country it was a land of fear and despair, with peasant groups meeting in secret, the armed police and military patrolling every road, terrorizing the poor at random. The people's only hope—Father Jean-Bertrand Aristide. When I returned from my first visit, I wrote: "This thin, frail, bird-like man is Aristide, the revolutionary priest? There must be some mistake. What is so dangerous about giving penicillin to the poor in the make-shift clinic he opened? In Haiti, one child dies every five minutes from malnutrition, dehydration, and diarrhea. What is so threatening about putting thin mattresses on concrete floors for hundreds of homeless boys in the old house he bought for street children?

One million people inhabit Port-au-Prince; 40,000 of them live in the streets. What is so frightening about teaching boys and girls to read and write in the classrooms he opened? In Haiti eighty percent of the population is illiterate. What is so revolutionary about running a clinic, an orphanage, a school?"

Only when Aristide opens his mouth do we understand. A fire-brand prophet, his words detonate dreams dormant for centuries in city slums and countryside shacks, setting peasant hearts aflame. He preaches human dignity. He demands equal distribution of wealth and land. He insists that the church divest itself of power and privilege and stand with the poor.

If it's true that dictatorships totter when one person dares to say NO, then Haiti's foundation is crumbling. In slumblock after slumblock the poor scribble the name, ARISTIDE, on public walls and fences and billboards. A poet once said, "Revolution only needs good dreamers who remember their dreams and the love of the people." Aristide has both. For this reason the soldiers shot at him in the night. For this reason the military tried to machete him. For this reason his church was fire bombed and torched. For this reason his order expelled him. For this reason he was stripped of his pulpit. For this reason Aristide is a dangerous man, a revolutionary priest. Certainly, 1989 was a dark time for Haiti and I expected Aristide and those who had hosted the Pax Christi delegation to be dead or in prison within the year.

But this is the scene from my second visit, just fifteen months later: A human wave of joy sweeps over Port-au-Prince. In slum section after slum section, the radio begins to record election results and the cry of the poor erupts in jubilation. Against the power of the United States government, against the threats of the Haitian elite and Duvalier cronies, against the might of the military, against the terror of the secret police, the death squads of Tonton Macoutes—against all these, this destitute, illiterate people held a free election and swept Titid, their beloved Father Aristide into the presidential palace. All of Port-au-Prince is awash with shouts of gladness.

On my third visit I represented Pax Christi International at the inauguration of President Jean-Bertrand Aristide. And what an inauguration invitation he issued. "Come," he said, "come you who are hungry, come to the banquet. All who have no money, come. All who are lame and sick. Come. Come to the presidential palace. You who have nothing are honored guests at the feast." And the poor came. And they came. And they came. Some hobbled on crutches, others crawled through the presidential gates on leg stubs, cautiously, proudly, they came to eat breakfast with their president.

So many came that they moved to the courtyard where—before the television cameras of the world—Aristide invited the poor to speak about their lives, their hopes for the future. A man without fingers or feet, a beggar who lived on the street, pleaded for a chance to own a bit of land. "Even without fingers," he said, "I can plant crops." "Come," Aristide said to the rich. "Come to the banquet. Bring your money and food. Give this man a chance. Give all of Haiti a chance.

12

Together we can build the new Jerusalem." Then, the new president of Haiti lifted a bowl filled with food, walked across the lawn, knelt in front of a woman going blind, and fed her breakfast.

Indeed the reign of God drew nearer and Mary's prayer that the lowly be filled with good things and the rich sent empty away seemed fulfilled.

And then...and then...the shattering events of September 1991—the ruthless military coup, the slaughter of the innocent, Aristide sent into exile, the violent and powerful triumphant, the bodies and dreams of the poor dashed against the rocks.

On the morning following the coup, when my community gathered to pray the psalms I could barely chant Psalm 12:

13

"For the poor who are oppressed and the needy who groan, I myself will arise," says God. "I will grant them the freedom for which they long." All my words on the length of God's love seemed facile and meaningless. But I did chant it, albeit half-heartedly and in a whisper. Is it true? And if it is true, when will it happen? When will God arise and grant the poor and oppressed the freedom for which they long?

Truly, only God knows. It is a faith response, then, not to be devastated by daily headline tragedies. One who fully grasps the length of God's love remembers always that the reign of God depends on God. All we can do is speak for life and leave the next sentence to a God of surprises, a God who writes straight with crooked lines.

All we can do is set our sights on the peaceable kingdom and do what we can to bring in God's reign—a glass of cold water to the weary, a word of comfort to the confused, a bowl of soup to the hungry, a letter of protest to the president, an act of resistance against the powerful, a life of solidarity with the poor. All we can do is the right thing because it is the right thing to do.

All we can do is detach ourselves from results and trust that God will accomplish God's purpose and plan in God's period of time.

All we can do is hold fast to the promise given by God to Dame Julian of Norwich: All shall be well, all shall be well, yes, all manner of things shall be well.

PART 4:

BREADTH OF
GOD'S LOVE

Gandhi hinted at the breadth of God's love when he wrote: "If you don't find God in the very next person you meet, it is a waste of time to look for God any further."

For me, the breadth of God's love is synonymous with all-embracing. To grasp fully this love poured out and overflowing is to open our arms wide that the suffering of the world may come in; is to answer each stranger's knock with "Blessed be God"; is to walk with the poor and hungry and call each one by name.

To make visible this love beyond measure is to be about abundance, is to be about largesse, is to be like the old woman in this story:

Just before dawn a young person was walking down a deserted beach. In the distance he saw a frail old woman. As he approached the old woman, he saw her picking up starfish and throwing them back into the sea. The young man gazed in wonder as the old woman again and again threw the small starfish from the sand to the water. He asked her, "Why do you spend so much energy doing what seems to be a waste of time?" The old woman explained that the stranded starfish would die if left in the morning sun. "But there must be thousands of beaches and millions of starfish," explained the young man. "How can your effort make any difference?" The old woman looked down at the small starfish in her hand and as she threw it to safety in the sea, she said, "It makes a difference to this one."

In this old woman we find a portrait of the breadth of God's love. Try not to think of her as someone simply doing an act of love, like giving drink to a thirsty person, or handing a slice of bread to a hungry child. Imagine her instead as one whose entire life is absorbed by the pain of others, whose every waking hour is oriented towards relieving that pain.

Rather than a beach awash with stranded starfish think of a world filled with suffering children. And picture this woman so moved with pity at the sight that she spends herself doing what she can to help the victims, even if it means challenging systems that support such suffering.

Behold, in this old woman who throws starfish after starfish into the sea and gives life to those on the edge of despair and death, we recognize someone who grasps fully the breadth of God's love.

Like this old woman, we, too, are invited to be love unfailing. We, too, are asked to be "starthrowers," to fling star after star against the wide sky and brighten a dark and desolate world.

To become the breadth of God's love would seem unreachable were it not for sacred guides, people who have gone before us, who have searched for and found the Beloved and can show us the way. Scripture calls them the cloud of witnesses and the church refers to them as the communion of saints.

These are biblical figures like David, abandoning himself to praise and dancing naked before the ark; and Mary Magdalen pouring expensive perfume over Jesus' feet in an outrageous and extravagant gesture of love. These are mystics and poets like the Sufi Rumi who says of God, "I leapt from you and you devoured me," or Thomas Merton who says that if we could see with the eyes of God our problem would be that we would fall down and worship one another.

These are modern prophets like Dorothy Day—50 years of feeding the hungry, sheltering the homeless and saying NO to war—her life an outpouring of her favorite quote: "Love in action is a harsh and dreadful thing compared to love in dreams."

Or Daniel Berrigan—ah, Daniel Berrigan, a lovely lyric poem that I want to memorize. There are artists like Vincent

Van Gogh swimming in yellow sunflowers and starry, starry nights and Shug from the novel, *Color Purple*, praying to the God of purple flowers in a field somewhere.

There are contemporary martyrs like Martin Luther King, Jr., who held so fast to his dreams than even an assassin's bullet could not destroy it. Or the four women martyrs of El Salvador, their faithfulness to death so simply explained by Dorothy Kazel: "We wouldn't want to run out on the people...we wouldn't want to run out on the people."

Yes, in a Day, a King, a Kazel, we see reflected the breadth of God's love. "Touch men and women like these," Walter Burghardt writes, "and you will touch the stars, you will touch God." But observation and inspiration are not enough. If we want to grasp fully the breadth of God's love, we must imitate, we must practice being loving.

Make no mistake about it, the habit of love—like all habits—is something we learn. We will experience fully the breadth of God's love only by loving, only by bending down to help over and over again. To be kind and gentle through mean-spirited and hard-hearted days, to offer one's simple gifts to a broken world, to give of self with abandon, though there is no consolation, no evidence of good results and no end in sight, to keep courage and hope alive during the worst of times, is all we are asked to do, is everything we are asked to do.

"Do you want to be a saint, do you want to make visible the breadth of God's love" a mystic asks. "Then be kind, be kind, be kind."

PART 5

CONCLUSION

These are some limited thoughts on a spirituality of nonviolence, some attempts to bring logic to love, even though love, by its nature, leaps beyond and can never be contained by the rational and logical.

But how, you may ask, how does this happen? How does nonviolent love become the root and foundation of our lives?

Again, we look to our cloud of witnesses. Daily prayer and meditation; simplicity of life; service to others, especially the poor; nonviolent actions against injustice; building of human community; a commitment not to harm any living thing—all are integral to nonviolence, to becoming those beams of love that William Blake said we were put on earth to be.

In a world that depends on massive slaughter of civilians to settle conflicts; in a world held hostage by unimaginable and unparalleled weapons of war—nonviolence is a beacon of hope.

In a world where exploitation and injustice are the daily bread of two-thirds of humanity; in a world where three-fourths of the world's poor are women—nonviolence is a comet against a dark sky. In a world where neighbors shoot each other for parking spaces and children carry machine guns, not lunch boxes, to school; in a world where consumerism and overconsumption are robbing the next generation of healing sunlight and drinkable water—nonviolence is a star leading to life.

"A journey of a thousand miles begins with one step,"

observed Confucius. To open the Doorway to Peace is one small step, but a step nevertheless on the long spiritual journey of nonviolence, a step toward that time when we experience fully the height and depth, breadth and length of God's love.

Or, as an ancient story tells it: A seeker searched for years to know the secret of achievement and meaning in human life. One night in a dream the Holy One appeared, bearing the answer to the secret. The sage said simply, "Stretch out your hand and reach what you can." "No, it can't be that," said the seeker. "It must be something harder, something more satisfying to the human spirit." The sage replied softly, "You are right, it is something harder. It is this: Stretch out your hand and reach what you cannot."

Isn't that what the spirituality of nonviolence is all about? It challenges us to chance the Christ, to risk all we have on love, and to stretch out our hands to reach what we cannot. Only in the striving for a nonviolent spirituality will our restless spirits find meaning, only in the struggle for a nonviolent heart will our restless spirits be satisfied. Leo Rosten warned: "The purpose of life is to matter, to have it make a difference that you have lived at all." If you choose a life of nonviolence, if you enter the doorway to peace, your life will have a purpose. It will matter. It will matter to you and to others that you have been here at all.

My prayer for you is that you choose to make a difference, that you choose to hiss, but not to harm, that you choose to hear the Voice that calls you Beloved, that you choose to be compassion within compassion within compassion, that you choose right action, not results, that you choose to throw star after star against a dark sky, that you choose to stretch out your hand and reach what you cannot.

My prayer for you is that you choose to open the Doorway to Peace, and enter into the spirituality of Christian nonviolence.

LOVE BEYOND MEASURE:
A Spirituality of Nonviolence

Sessions

Compiled by: Michelle Balek, OSF, Marlene Bertke, OSB,
Jim Dinn and Anne McCarthy, OSB

SESSION 1:
DEPTH OF
GOD'S LOVE

OPENING PRAYER

(After a moment of
silence, light the Peace
Candle, displayed in a
prominent place.)

Song: "I Have Loved
You with an Everlasting
Love" (or similar song)

Scripture: Luke 15: 25-32

Meanwhile the elder son was out in the fields. As he neared
the house on his way home, he heard the sound of music and
dancing. When he called a servant and asked him the reason
for the dancing and the music, the servant replied, "Your
brother is home and your father has killed the fatted calf
because he has him back in good health." The son grew angry
at this and would not go into the house. So his father came out
and began to plead with him. In reply, the elder son said, "For
years now I have slaved for you. I never disobeyed one of
your orders, yet you never gave me so much as a kid goat to
celebrate with my friends. Then when this son of yours re-
turns after having gone through your property with loose
women, you kill the fatted calf for him."

"My son," replied the father, "you are with me always and
everything I have is yours. But we had to celebrate and rejoice.
This brother of yours was dead and has come back to life; he
was lost and is found!"

Short Pause

Facilitator: We speak and God responds. (One person can speak God's responses.)

All: We persevere in what we see as our duty, sometimes generously, sometimes grudgingly, thinking we need to prove ourselves or earn your approval.
God: I always love you.

All: When we fail in our efforts, we feel guilty and discouraged; when we succeed, we feel proud.
God: I always love you.

All: Sometimes others look on us with suspicion, or envy, or amusement, or hatred—and we feel hurt.
God: I always love you.

All: Sometimes we look on others with suspicion, or envy, or amusement, or hatred—and we feel justified.
God: I always love you.

All: Sometimes our life feels monotonous, or exciting, or productive, or overwhelming—and we think our value goes up or down with our mood.
God: I always love you.

All: Sometimes we forget you, ignore you, question you, or even oppose you.
God: I always love you.

God: No matter what you do or don't do, no matter how you feel about yourself or how anyone else feels about you, whether you remember me or forget me, I want you to know in the very fibers of your being that I always love you.

Song: "I Have Loved You with an Everlasting Love" (refrain only)

PRIMARY READING

Love Beyond Measure, Part 1 (begins on page 1)

Questions

1. Share the passage that most affected you.

2. From your perspective, how compatible is "hissing" with nonviolence? Do you hiss?

3. What is the connection between God loving you and your ability to live nonviolently?

4. What were the circumstances the last time you came face to face with the violence inside yourself?

5. When have you felt unworthy to be a peacemaker? What helps you cope with this feeling?

6. How do you recover or preserve your sense of God's love for you, your lovability?

SCRIPTURE READING
Luke 15: 25-32

Questions

1. In the parable, what would it take for the "faithful" daughter or son to feel loved and appreciated? Focus especially on aspects that the daughter or son can control.

2. In your own experience, does the treatment of a sister or brother, a co-worker, or another community member ever expose a darker side of your own attitudes?

3. Imagine and describe the return of the prodigal son if the older son were truly comfortable with himself, truly loved himself and felt loved.

4. If the older daughter or son has no change of heart, how will it affect their potential as a peacemaker within the family? Outside the family?

RELATED READINGS

Reading 1

For a rather small number of people, conversion is an extraordinary, almost catastrophic, act in which everything is turned topsy-turvy, after which nothing is ever again the same. The most obvious examples are Paul, the persecutor turned apostle; Francis, the debonair young courtier become poor man; Martin Luther, a sin-obsessed monk transformed into a radical reformer. But for most of us, as for Dorothy Day, conversion is a lifelong process. She always spoke of herself as "on pilgrimage."...

Reduced to its simplest dimensions, this day-in, day-out conversion is a renewal of one's humble acceptance of God's forgiveness. An Anglican bishop, Dr. Peter Walker, put it beautifully in his enthronement sermon in the great Cathedral Church at Ely in East Anglia. He described how he and his wife had been on a brief holiday in Tuscany and had been urged by friends to stop and see a quite remarkable 15th century church with some paintings by one of the Bellinis. As they walked up the nave of the church, the bishop reported, his eyes were drawn to a piece of brown wrapping paper pinned to the front of the pulpit. On it were written the words Ora, Dio ti ama! ("God loves you now!")

It is precisely this awareness, humbly appropriated into one's life, that is the foundation stone of the conversion process. If we truly believe that God loves us now for what we are now, no strings attached, then we cannot but be embarked on that conversion of heart and manners which is the essence of

the response to the invitation of Jesus.
—from *Mirrors of God* by Joseph W. Goetz, St. Anthony Messenger Press,
Cincinnati, Ohio.

Questions

1. If the older son or daughter in the parable came to Goetz
for advice, what advice do you think he would give?

2. In your life, do you find dramatic conversion or multiple
daily conversions?

3. Are there messages in your own life about God's love that
you can share? Are there some that you have been overlook-
ing or undervaluing?

4. Are there ways to increase your sensitivity to God's love
messages? Are there ways you can help others receive their
messages?

Reading 2

For the past several years, I have been a hospice nurse,
caring for people who are dying....

I have been shocked by the number of Christian men and
women who come to their deathbeds knowing nothing about
the God of love and mercy. They have known instead the
Judge of impossible standards, and they have been, naturally
enough, afraid to meet that God.

There is no way to challenge such ideas with words. The
only way I can challenge judgmental, harsh notions of God is
by loving.

I do that by faithful and loving care of the body, which
becomes increasingly more difficult to care for and often
repulsive. If I remain loving and faithful to that task until the
end, the patient has a new and life-giving experience of God....

I have seen people reach the point of conscious and deliber-
ate surrender, and I have learned this: they do not surrender
to death. They surrender to love, love that is ordinary and
human. When they surrender to that love, they surrender to

God, and they die peacefully. But that ordinary human love must be there.

Through care of the body, this love is my contribution.

—from "Prayer of the Flesh," by Eve Kavanagh; *The Other Side*, May-June, 1993. Reprinted with permission: The Other Side, 300 West Apsley Street, Philadelphia, PA 19144. (Subscription: $29.50/year.)

Questions

1. Does your image of God affect your attitudes about dying? How? What does this have to do with nonviolence?

2. Which reading in this section of the book helps you most to renew your awareness of God's love for you? Kownacki? The parable? Goetz? Kavanagh?

3. If you are discussing this in a group, what insight from someone else in the group has most helped your focus on God's love?

CLOSING PRAYER

Facilitator: Let us pray.

All: O God, your love underlies every aspect of our lives.
Deeper than our minds or memories can fathom,
beneath every aspect of all human existence,
every aspect of everything that ever has been or will be—
            your love is present.
Teach us to accept and celebrate your love
for each of us
so that we can effectively serve others with love.
We pray in a spirit of faith. Amen.

Song: "On Eagle's Wings" (or similar song)

SESSION 2:
HEIGHT OF
GOD'S LOVE

OPENING PRAYER

(After a moment of silence, light the Peace Candle, displayed in a prominent place.)

Song: "Eye Has Not Seen"

Scripture: Luke 6: 27-37

But to you who are willing to hear, I say, love your enemies, do good to those who hate you, bless those who curse you, pray for those who mistreat you. To the person who strikes you on one cheek, offer the other one as well, and from the person who takes your cloak, do not withhold even your tunic. Give to everyone who asks of you, and from the one who takes what is yours, do not demand it back. Do to others as you would have them do to you. For if you love those who love you, what credit is that to you? Even sinners love those who love them. And if you do good to those who do good to you, what credit is that to you? Even sinners do the same. If you lend money to those from whom you expect repayment, what credit is that to you? Even sinners lend to sinners, and get back the same amount. But rather, love your enemies and do good to them, and lend expecting nothing back; then your reward will be great and you will be children of the Most High, for the Holy One is kind to the ungrateful and the wicked. Be merciful, just as God is merciful.

Stop judging and you will not be judged. Stop condemning and you will not be condemned. Forgive and you will be forgiven.

Reader 1: My sister was one of the women religious murdered in Liberia.

Reader 2: My 18-year-old son was killed by a drunk driver while he was out collecting groceries for the Food Bank.

All: God, your command is hard—to love as you do, passionately and without reserve. Judgment is not our task, for we do not know what is in the heart of another. We look to the example of those great lovers who have gone before us.

Reader 3: Give us the fire of Abraham who loved God so much that he was willing to sacrifice God's promise of descendants through Isaac.

All: For Abraham's courageous love we give thanks.

Reader 1: Give us the selfless love of Esther who saved her people from persecution and death.

All: For Esther's love of her people we give thanks.

Reader 2: Give us the outrageous love of Jesus who gave his life for sinners.

All: For Jesus' redemptive love we give thanks.

Reader 3: For the transforming love of Martin Luther King, Jr. who dreamed of a nonviolent world.

All: For Martin's nonviolent love we give thanks.

Reader 1: Give us the fearless love of Ita, Dorothy, Maura and Jean; of Romero and all the modern martyrs who refused to be tryannized by ruthless governments.

All: For martyrs' love we give thanks.

Facilitator: Let us pray.

All: Holy and Compassionate One, we give you thanks
for sharing your love with us in the persons of your
saints. Their undying love is an example for us who
are deadened by war and hate and greed.
Give us the courage to go beyond our self-imposed
limits to love as they have, freely and openly, without
counting the cost. We ask this of you in the name of
Jesus, our brother.

Song: "Eye Has Not Seen" (refrain only)

PRIMARY READING

Love Beyond Measure, Part 2 (begins on page 6)

Questions

1. *"We become like the God we adore."* Who is the God you
adore? Be specific in your description. Can you name any
ways that you are becoming like this God?

2. Have you ever watched someone absorb hatred and violence without striking back? How did that experience impact
you, influence you?

3. Pray with Bishop Theas the prayer that Jesus taught us—
what word would you substitute for **Germany?**

4. Thomas Merton said, in words similar to Etty Hillesum's:
"Instead of loving what you think is peace, love other men
and women and love God above all else. Instead of hating all
the people you think are warmongers, hate the appetites and
disorders in your own soul which are the causes of war."
What changes would come about in your life if you really
tried to do this?

5. Have you ever experienced the "God of mercy within mercy
within mercy"? What might our world look like if **this** were

the God preached in our churches and faithfully followed by believers?

6. *"To experience fully the height of God's love I must swim in this ocean of compassion."* When was the last time you were on the receiving end of compassionate love? When was the last time you shared compassionate love?

SCRIPTURE READING
Luke 6: 27-37

Questions

1 *"Lend expecting nothing back."* Could this be applied to the situation of Third World debt? These countries are being strangled by paying the interest on their debt—without a cent going toward the principal. In most cases, the principal has actually been paid several times over through the interest payments. Should US banks and other financial institutions now cancel the debt?

2. *"From the one who takes what is yours, do not demand it back."* Could this scripture passage be used to justify non-action when someone steals $10 from your pocket or when one country invades another and seizes territory? How do you understand this scripture? To what does it call you?

RELATED READINGS

Reading 1

In the early 1980s the Guatemalan peasants were being massa- cred by the military. Many of them fled to Mexico but others fled to very remote places in the mountains and jungles of Guatemala where they lived with no contact with the outer world. They became

*known as Communities of Population in Resistance, CPRs. The
army continued to bomb them, raid their small villages, burn and
pillage. They were constantly on the move fleeing the army.*

*Curt Grove, one of the Pax Christi representatives who partici-
pated in the first "walk-in" to the CPRs tells of this experience
during that visit:*

The most profound happening of the entire time for me was
the homily given by Marcellino, a lay catechist of the CPR
Cabá community. He spoke so eloquently about nonviolence
and forgiveness.

"We don't want to bear arms because we don't consider
anyone our enemy. We know that we are all brothers and
sisters, even those who persecute us. The same blood flows
through our veins. We all live in the same country. We're all
exploited, humiliated, marginalized.

"Forgiving those who do evil to us does not mean to let
them continue to do evil, but to teach them to change their
attitudes and their lives. It doesn't mean, 'I forgive you for the
evil you've done to me, but if you want to continue to do evil,
that's up to you.' Jesus teaches us the way and then forgives
us. First he teaches us the path we must walk, and we have to
do the same to our brothers and sisters who persecute us. We
want to show them the evil they have done and the path of
justice, the path of peace, the path of love.

"If our hearts had been full of hatred and bitterness we
would have taken up arms to take away the arms of those
who massacred our people. The word of God gives us
strength and our faith gives us courage to continue to struggle
in love to obtain our rights. We do not want them to be our
enemies; we want to be united with them again.

"...when we try to put it into practice, the word of God is
very simple..."

—*Pax Christi Magazine*, Vol. XVIII, No. 2, Summer, 1993

Questions

1. "We do not want them to be our enemies; we want to be
united with them again." Is this your attitude when you are
experiencing enmity toward another person? Toward national

enemies? What do you do when feelings of "getting even" spring up inside you?

2. Do you find yourself willing to "show them the evil they have done," or do you usually take what seems to be the easier path of simply turning away? Give one example of each.

Reading 2

John Oliver Killens states in his book, *Black Man's Burden*, "...there is no dignity for me in allowing another person to spit on me with impunity. There is no dignity for them or for me. There is only sickness, and it will beget an even greater sickness. It degrades me and brutalizes them. Moreover, it encourages them in their bestiality."
—from *Black Man's Burden* by John Oliver Killens, Random House, Inc., New York, NY, 1965.

Questions

1. How do you deal honestly with the reality that nonviolence is sometimes preached to people who are being subjected to violence, especially the more subtle structural violence.

2. How do you deal honestly with concerns about passivity being seen as nonviolence?

CLOSING PRAYER

Facilitator: Let us pray.

All: God of Love that soars to heights unimaginable,
            be with us.
        Guide us on your prophetic path of mercy.
        Give us compassionate and forgiving hearts
            that your Reign of Love may come.

May we be rooted in you,
    that our love, too, may gently soar—
        to heights we never believed possible.

Song: "Eye Has Not Seen" (refrain only)

SESSION 3:
LENGTH OF
GOD'S LOVE

OPENING PRAYER

(After a moment of
silence, light the Peace
Candle, displayed in a
prominent place.)

Mantra:
(Repeat three times. Can
be sung with gesture.)

May my mind think no harm,
May my lips speak no harm,
May my hands do no harm.
May the children of tomorrow
  bless the work I offer.
—Mary Lou Kownacki, OSB

Scripture: Luke 4:16-21

When Jesus came to Nazareth where he had been brought
up he entered the synagogue on the Sabbath as he usually did.
He stood up to read and they handed him the book of the
prophet Isaiah.

Jesus then unrolled the scroll and found the place where it
is written:

"The spirit of God is upon me. He has anointed me to bring
good news to the poor, to proclaim liberty to captives and to
give new sight to the blind; to free the oppressed and an-
nounce God's year of mercy.

Jesus then rolled up the scroll, gave it to the attendant and
sat down, while the eyes of all in the synagogue were fixed on
him. Then he said to them, "Today these prophetic words
come true even as you listen."

Short Pause

Facilitator: Let us pray.

All: Today, may these prophetic words come true even as we listen.

Voice 1: For Indigenous peoples in Guatemala
Voice 2: For people in China and East Timor
Voice 3: For people in Somalia and the Sudan
Voice 4: For the people of the former Yugoslavia
Voice 5: For Native Americans and African Americans in the United States.

All: Today, may these prophetic words come true even as we listen.

Voice 1: For the homeless
Voice 2: For single mothers bound in poverty
Voice 3: For gay men and lesbian women
Voice 4: For children in the womb
Voice 5: For women and men and adolescents on death row

All: Today, may these prophetic words come true even as we listen.

(Repeat mantra three times.)

PRIMARY READING

Love Beyond Measure, Part 3 (begins on page 10)

Questions
1. What struck you in this reading? Explain.

2. Do you think it is true that dictatorships totter when one person dares to say NO. Why or why not?

3. Mary Lou holds up President Aristide as a model of solidarity. Can you think of others? Have you seen anything from US leaders that is comparable?

4. *"A thousand years in God's sight are as yesterday that is past."* Mary Lou asks, "With this view of time, how can one despair?" Think of the last letter you wrote or phone call you made to a political or religious leader. Did you have expectations? What was your view of time?

5. *"God writes straight with crooked lines."* Recall one instance in your life when this proved true.

RELATED READINGS

Reading 1

Quasars, scientists teach, are ten trillion times more brilliant than ordinary stars such as the sun. They are so bright that they can be observed at distances more than 10 billion light years away from earth. Some of the ones we see, in fact, have been dead for several billion years and their light is just reaching the earth. When nothing you do seems to prosper, to take root, to grow, quasars teach us not to despair. Some light comes later, long after it first dared to gleam.
—Joan Chittister, OSB, Monastic Way, May, 1993, Benetvision, Erie, PA

Questions

1. It is easy to get caught up in working for results. What is not helpful about that? Are there ways that working for results is helpful?

2. Can you explain how trusting in God's time is different from passivity? Can you give a concrete example of each from your own life?

Reading 2

Clementine Chism Barfield started Save Our Sons and Daughters (SOSAD) after two sons, ages 15 and 16 were shot in 1986. Clementine felt the need to go beyond mourning for her sons and to work to stop the violence among children. SOSAD is credited in helping to reduce youth homicide in Detroit by 25% over the past three years. Clementine Chism Barfield has created a national movement to save the children.

Questions

1. Have you ever known of personal tragedy to hold the seeds of new initiatives? Do faith and prayer have a role in this?

2. Can you share an example in which your personal pain helped you cross the line to help others cope with similar pain?

SCRIPTURE READING
Luke 4: 16-21

Questions

1. Think of a situation in the **world.** In what ways are Jesus' prophetic words from Isaiah evidenced there? In what ways have you contributed or supported? In what ways is the message from Isaiah still awaiting fullness?

2. Think of a situation in your **city, town or local community.** In what ways are Jesus' prophetic words from Isaiah evidenced there? In what ways have you contributed or supported? In what ways is the message from Isaiah still awaiting fullness?

3. Think of a situation in your **family or community.** In what ways are Jesus' prophetic words from Isaiah evidenced there? In what ways have you contributed or supported? In what ways is the message from Isaiah still awaiting fullness?

CLOSING PRAYER

Facilitator: Listen to this message from Thomas Merton, the monk of Gethsemani, written to a young activist. Listen as if the message were addressed to you.

"Do not depend on the hope of results. When you are doing the sort of work you have taken on, essentially an apostolic work, you may have to face the fact that your work will be apparently worthless and even achieve no result at all, if not perhaps results opposite to what you expect. As you get used to this idea, you start more and more to concentrate not on the results, but on the value, the rightness, the truth of the work itself. And there too a great deal has to be gone through, as gradually you struggle less and less for an idea and more and more for specific people. The range tends to narrow down, but it gets much more real. In the end, it is the reality of personal relationships that saves everything."
—Thomas Merton, "Letter to a Young Activist," *Peacemaking Day by Day, Book 1*, Pax Christi USA

Mantra: (from opening prayer, repeated three times with gesture.)

SESSION 4:
BREADTH OF
GOD'S LOVE

OPENING PRAYER

(After a moment of silence, light the Peace Candle, displayed in a prominent place.)

Song: "Ubi Caritas" (or similar song that all will know)

Scripture: Hebrews 13: 1-3, 5-8

Love always. Do not neglect to show hospitality, for by that means some have entertained angels without knowing it. Be as mindful of prisoners as if you were sharing their imprisonment, and of the ill-treated as of yourselves, for you may yet suffer as they do. Do not love money but be content with what you have, for God has said, "I will never desert you, nor will I forsake you." Thus we may say with confidence:

"God is my helper, I will not be afraid; what can others do to me?"

Remember your leaders who spoke the word of God to you; consider how their lives ended, and imitate their faith. Jesus Christ is the same yesterday, today, and forever.

Short Pause

LITANY
 (Facilitator begins the litany; everyone responds.)
 To the Haitian refugees...*let us open our arms wide.*
 To those trapped in the cycle of poverty...
 To the victims of violence...

To the homeless and hungry...
To the nameless and forgotten...
To the Serbs and the Croats and the Muslims...
To the victims and perpetrators of abuse...
To the stranger and alien in our midst...
To those on the edge of despair and death...
To the communion of saints...
To the mystics, poets and artists...
To the prophets who disrupt our comfort...
To the prisoner and the ill-treated...
To the friend and the enemy...
To the Palestinians and Israelis...
To the Moslems, Jews and Christians...
To the displaced and disappeared...
To the victims of torture...

All: Prayer of Jesus: Mother/Father God, who are in heaven...

PRIMARY READING

Love Beyond Measure, Part 4 (begins on page 15)

Questions

1. With which phrase, idea or image in this section do you most resonate? Which disturbed you the most? Why?

2. In what way(s) are you a "starthrower" shedding light in the darkness?

3. Name the "Sacred Guides" in your life. Why do they appeal to you? Which of their qualities would you like to incorporate more fully into your life? What is the danger in viewing your Sacred Guides as "extraordinary" people who do/have done "extraordinary" things?

4. The current "War on Drugs" campaign takes a violent

stance/attack on the problem of drug abuse and trafficking. What would happen if we "waged compassion" instead of war on this problem? How can you open your arms to this suffering?

5. We live in a "throw-away" society. How does this attitude toward "things" begin to extend to people, and what violence does it do to individual people and to society as a whole? How can you open your arms to this suffering?

RELATED READINGS

Reading 1

I am the mayfly metamorphosing in the
    surface of the river,
  and I am the bird which, when spring comes,
    arrives in time to eat the mayfly.

I am the frog swimming happily in the clear water
    of a pond,
  and I am also the grass-snake who,
    approaching in silence,
    feeds itself on the frog.

I am the child in Uganda, all skin and bones,
    my legs as thin as bamboo sticks,
  and I am the arms merchant, selling deadly
    weapons to Uganda.

I am the 12-year-old girl, refugee on a small boat,
    who throws herself into the ocean after
    being raped by a sea pirate,
  and I am the pirate, my heart not yet capable
    of seeing and loving....

My joy is like spring, so warm it makes flowers bloom
    in all walks of life.

My pain is like a river of tears, so full it fills up
    the four oceans.

Please call me by my true names,
    so I can hear all my cries and my laughs at once,
    so I can see that my joy and pain are one.
Please call me by my true names, so I can wake up,
    and so the door of my heart can be left open,
    the door of compassion.

—Reprinted with permission from *Call Me By My True Names: The Collected Poems of Thich Nhat Hanh,* by Thich Nhat Hanh, Parallax Press, Berkeley, CA, 1993.

Reading 2

In Spring 1993, a religious cult was attacked by the FBI in an effort to prevent what was feared to be abuse of children in their compound by the cult leader.

The shoot-out and siege (of the Branch Davidians in the Ranch Apocalypse compound) in Waco, Texas have raised the issue of religious fanaticism in the mind of America....When such violent fanaticism rears its ugly head, a standard response gushes forth from the media and is present, implicitly or explicitly, in most public discussions on the issue. This is the conventional wisdom: It is dangerous to become too religious. The best advice is to stay as "normal" and mainstream as possible.

Religious commitment itself becomes suspect, especially if it is strong and life-defining, moves away from dominant cultural values, and creates community. The answer to any kind of religious commitment seems to be secularism, or at least religion with huge doses of moderation, allowing us to swallow most of society's secular consensus. But the problem with the cultic violence in Texas...is not that it's too religious. On the contrary, these militant fundamentalists are not religious enough. In reality, they are not religious at all....True religion should not be blamed for violent fanaticism done in the name of religion. Yet the religious community could and should take responsibility for trying to resolve such conflicts peacefully. Wouldn't that be in keeping with our true vocation?

What might have happened if church leaders and members from Waco encircled the Ranch Apocalypse compound with an unarmed vigil of prayer, dialogue, discernment, and nonviolent conflict resolution? I don't know. But what different dynamic might have been possible if a nonviolent army of Christian peacemakers had surrounded the place instead of flak-jacketed federal agents with their guns blazing and hungry reporters with their cameras whirring? That might have been the most truly religious response of all to "religious fanaticism."

—from "Giving Religion a Bad Name," by Jim Wallis, Sojourners Magazine, Vol. 22, No. 4, May 1993

Questions

1. With which phrase, idea, or image did you most resonate? Which disturbed you the most? Why?

2. What is the wisdom of Thich Nhat Hanh's idea of recognizing both the peaceful and the violent within ourselves? What are your true names?

3. It is estimated that currently there are 200,000,000 handguns owned privately in the U.S. What do these numbers tell us about the "need" for violence to make us "feel" safe? Is this true security? How can you open your arms to this suffering?

4. In Mary Lou's story, she relates that the young man considers the old woman's actions a "waste of time," and quite crazy. Do the ideas offered by Jim Wallis seem "crazy" to you? Would they seem crazy to you if, because someone else enacted them, you were the one spared violence/death?

SCRIPTURE READING
Hebrews 13:1-3, 5-8

Questions

1. The "hospitality" in this passage is more than merely offering lodging and a meal. It calls us to share in the imprisonment and ill- treatment of others. How is this gospel call of hospitality related to nonviolence?

2. What are the fears that prevent us from "loving always"?

3. What does this passage say to us about nonviolence and nonaction?

4. How does being "content with what you have" relate to "loving always"? (i.e. Reflect on how our US lifestyle is often maintained at the expense of third world peoples. Think in terms of clothes, fuel, etc.)

5. Who are the everyday "leaders" from among your family, neighbors, co-workers, etc. whose faith we are called to imitate today?

CLOSING PRAYER

Facilitator: Let us pray.

All: God of Love Beyond Measure,
we hear your call to open our arms wide
to let the suffering of the world
come into our lives.
Your call both frightens and invites us.
And we cannot remain passive
in the midst of the challenge.

We desire to live your love with total abandon;
>without counting the cost
>or the rewards.

We long to be "starthrowers"
>who care deeply for each one of your
>precious creatures;
>and who choose
>to make a difference where we can.

Give us the strength and wisdom, we pray,
>to enter this unending dance of love,
>every day, every hour, every moment,
>everywhere.   Amen.

Ritual:

Slowly pass the Peace Candle from person to person around the group, holding it briefly before passing it on. While holding it, each person is invited to name a person, group or situation that they would like to embrace more fully with a Love Beyond Measure. (This naming can be done in the silence of one's heart if this is more comfortable.)

Song: "Ubi Caritas" (or similar song)

SESSION 5:
CONCLUSION

OPENING PRAYER

(preferably done in a dark-
ened room)

All: God of
Love Beyond Measure,
  we gather together
    in your name
  seeking the Doorway
    to Peace.

(Leader lights the Peace Candle.)

  We know this is a long journey,
    one we have only just started
    and must start anew each day.
  We trust in your abiding presence
    to help guide our steps into the
    height and depth,
    breadth and length
    of your love.
  May we ever keep stretching out our hands
    to reach what we cannot.

(Each reader in turn lights a small candle from the Peace Candle, while reading their section. The readers should be scattered throughout the group.)

Reader 1: Nonviolence is a beacon of hope.

Reader 2: Nonviolence is a comet against a dark sky.

Reader 3: Nonviolence is a star leading to life.

Song: "We Are the Light of the World" (refrain only)

Scripture: Matthew 5:14-16

You are the light of the world. A city set on a hill cannot be hidden. People do not light a lamp and then put it under a bushel basket. They set it on a stand where it gives light to all in the house. In the same way, your light must shine before all so that they may see the goodness in your acts and give praise to God.

Short Pause

All:
I am only one, but I am one.
I cannot do everything, but I can do something.
What I can do, I ought to do,
and what I ought to do, by the grace of God,
I will do.
—Edward Everett Hale

Song: "We Are the Light of the World" (refrain only)

PRIMARY READING

Love Beyond Measure
Go back to the beginning of the book and re-read Mary Lou's essay, from start to finish, including the conclusion.

Questions

1. What new insights about nonviolence have you gained? What was reaffirmed for you?

2. Mary Lou lists the following six things as integral to non-violence. What is one concrete step/action you can take

(locally and/or globally) in each area to grow in the spirituality of nonviolence? (Some possibilities are listed.)

a. Daily prayer and meditation:
*Incorporate the headline stories from the newspaper into your daily prayer.
*Pray for a person you call "enemy."

b. Simplicity of life:
*Commit yourself/family/community to give creative alternative gifts at celebrations.
*Schedule regularly an inventory of your possessions and your needs.
What will you not purchase? What will you give away? What will you treasure?

c. Service to others, especially the poor:
*Interact regularly with children, the elderly, people with disabilities, those who are poor. Let your life be changed by the relationships.
*Volunteer time and talent in prison visitations and ministry.

d. Nonviolent actions against injustice:
*Write letters to your congress people in support of gun control legislation (Brady Bill).
*Join and promote local efforts for adequate representation of minorities in juries, police and fire departments, school boards, etc.

e. Building of human community:
*Commit yourself/group to participate in a dismantling racism/sexism workshop series (work with others to sponsor such workshops in your area if none have been initiated).
*Participate in (and/or help organize) conflict resolution programs in your area.

f. Commitment to not harm any living thing:
*Raise your awareness of environmental issues and

environmental spirituality by reading current
literature/viewing videos on these.
*Defend someone from name-calling or attacks—
especially someone with whom you disagree.

SCRIPTURE READING
Matthew 5:14-16

Questions

1. We are living in a very violent world and time. What is the comfort and challenge of this particular passage for you?

2. In simplified scientific terms, light is energy. Re-read this passage substituting "energy" for "light." What new insights does this shed for you in our world today?

RELATED READINGS

Reading 1

...What has not changed is the systemic and pervasive character of racism in the US and the condition of life for the majority of black people. In fact, these conditions have gotten worse. Racism originates in domination and provides the social rationale and philosophical justification for debasing, degrading and doing violence to people on the basis of color. Many have pointed out how racism is sustained by both personal attitudes and structural forces. Racism can be brutally overt or invisibly institutional, or both. Its scope extends to every level and area of human psychology, society and culture.....

The resurgence of more overt forms of white racism and violence is quite foreboding as yet another occasion when the discontented alienation of poor whites is displaced and expressed against blacks instead of at the system that oppresses them both and has always sought to turn them against each other....

All white people in the US have benefited from the structure of racism, whether or not they have ever committed a racist act, uttered a racist word, or had a racist thought (as unlikely as that is). Just as surely as blacks suffer in a white society because they are black, whites benefit because they are white. And if whites have profited from a racist structure, they must try to change it.

—from "The Legacy of White Racism," by Jim Wallis, *America's Original Sins: A Study Guide on White Racism*, Sojourners, Box 29272, Washington, DC 20017.

Questions

1. If you had the opportunity to address a group of "skin heads," the neo-Nazi white supremacist groups who are surfacing in frightening numbers, what would you say to them?

2. Can you name three ways in which you have benefited from the structure of racism? Three ways in which people of color suffer from the same structures? What blinds us to systemic violence?

3. In what ways are sexism and racism similar?

Reading 2

Women In Black is an informal movement of women that had its beginning in Israel with women standing in vigil throughout Israel to protest the occupation and the attendant violence. Women in Black Against War began on the streets of Belgrade in October 1991.

Women In Black stand every Wednesday, from 3:30 to 4:30 pm—the time of the local rush hour—in front of the Student Cultural Center of Belgrade in order to express our disapproval of the ongoing war in Croatia. The Belgrade group was joined by WIB from the neighboring town of Pancevo and today these two groups work together.

The presence of women on the streets draws sharp attention to the women's side of the war. Our presence provokes diverse reactions from the passers-by. Some try to ignore our existence; they turn their heads and walk on by. Others—a rather small group of women—feel good, encouraged, and they stop to talk and get more information. The most unpleasant reactions come from nationalist men who say: "Idle whores of Izetbegovic and Tudjman." "Traitors to the Serbian nation!" "Serbia is not at war; go protest to the Croats and Muslims."

Women in Black participate in many peace demonstrations. We took part in the "Anti-War Marathon," a forum of discussion that lasted for two months. At that time we also held candle vigils every night in front of the Serbian parliament and these continued for five months under the banner, "Solidarity with all those who rebel against the war." We were active in collecting signatures for the referendum against forced mobilization.

Last April, Women in Black participated in a big anti-war rally, "Don't Count On Us," a protest against the militarization of Bosnia.

A project we call "Listening" will take place in the village Banatski Brestovac, Vojvodina, where there are ethnic problems between Muslims and Serbs. In this project, women will be there to listen to other women's testimonies and try to set an example of listening to each other's experiences. The project will be developed together with women from the village.

—from the Women In Black national newsletter, No. 5, Spring 1993

Questions

1. Can you relate to these women? Can we in the US learn from these people-to-people movements protesting the war-making policies of their government and military leaders?

2. In Guatemala, CONAVIGUA, the organization of widows, began a campaign to end forced conscription and to honor conscientious objection. They are selling T-shirts emblazoned with these messages. Would you walk down the streets of

Guatemala City wearing such a shirt? In what ways is this comparable to Women In Black?

Reading 3

In the early 1990s, as violence flared in the Persian Gulf, Haiti, the Middle East, Central America, Somalia, Bosnia..., the peace movement struggled to find an appropriate alternative to the violent response followed by government leaders. "Peace Missions," such as the one described here, captured the imagination and focused the energy of those dedicated to nonviolent solutions to violent situations.

"We Share One Peace" is the name of a nonviolent action for peace in Bosnia-Herzegovina. The aim of this initiative, which is supported by Pax Christi Italy, is to contribute both to a peaceful solution of the armed conflict and to the real respect of the human rights of the people and groups involved in the conflict. The participants are going to set up a peace camp with groups of 60-80 people, each group staying for a period of one or two weeks, to ensure a stable presence in war-torn Sarajevo for several months. The aim is to share the suffering and problems caused by the war and to bring solidarity and moral support.

Questions

1. What are the pros and cons of nonviolent intervention in violent situations? Can you see a use for such a peace mission in other countries? In our own country?

2. What are the implications of such nonviolenct interventions in more familiar local settings, such as response to violence in classrooms, neighborhoods, and homes?

CLOSING PRAYER SERVICE

Song: "World Peace Prayer" (Refrain only)

Prayer:

All: O God, we want to choose a life of nonviolence.
　Help us to hiss, but not to harm;
　to hear the Voice that calls us Beloved;
　to be compassion within compassion within compassion;

　to choose right action, not results;
　to throw star after star against a dark sky;
　to stretch out our hands and reach what we cannot.

　Give us the strength and courage
　to not only believe, but to act;
　to recognize our own participation in violence and our
　　need for conversion;
　to challenge the unjust and violent structures of our day;

　to gather, time and again, around the table of dialogue;
　to create and promote peaceful alternatives wherever
　　we are;
　to continue to be a voice and witness of nonviolence.

　Our journey through the Doorway to Peace
　　begins with the step we choose to take today.
　Be with us. Guide us.
　Love us into your Love Beyond Measure.　Amen.

Have a small candle for each one in the group. Invite each person to come forward and light their candle from the Peace Candle. As it is lit, each is invited, if they are comfortable in doing so, to share one step they want to take toward nonviolence. You can use the following, or similar statement:
　I choose to make a difference in our world by...
(If someone prefers not to voice this aloud, they may simply say:
　I choose to make a difference in our world today.
Or they may light their candle in silence.)
Your group may choose to make the **Vow of Nonviolence**
(page 57)

Song: "World Peace Prayer"

A Vow of Nonviolence

One step that many have found useful in their journey toward disarming one's heart is that of taking the Vow of Nonviolence. Such a gesture signifies an explicit rejection of violence and a turning toward unconditional love.

This is a private vow, a personal commitment. It is not regulated by authority and does not carry any canonical obligation. The vow can be made for a specified time, perhaps a year. It may be renewed annually but some may wish to make a lifetime commitment.

The Vow of Nonviolence is meant to be freeing, not a burden of guilt. It implies a process toward a goal, not an overnight attainment of a nonviolent heart.

Such a private, devotional vow has a solid base in tradition—they have been taken by Christians for centuries.

Vow of Nonviolence

Recognizing the violence in my own heart, yet trusting in the goodness and mercy of God, I vow for one year to practice the nonviolence of Jesus who taught us in the Sermon on the Mount:

Blessed are the peacemakers, for they shall be called the sons and daughters of God.... You have learned how it was said, 'You must love your neighbor and hate your enemy,' but I say to you, 'Love your enemies and pray for those who persecute you. In this way you will be daughters and sons of your Creator in heaven.

Before God the Creator and the Sanctifying Spirit, I vow to carry out in my life the love and example of Jesus
   • by striving for peace within myself and seeking to be a peacemaker in my daily life;
   • by accepting suffering rather than inflicting it;
   • by refusing to retaliate in the face of provocation and violence;
   • by persevering in nonviolence of tongue and heart;

• by living conscientiously and simply so that I do not deprive others of the means to live;

• by actively resisting evil and working nonviolently to abolish war and the causes of war from my own heart and from the face of the earth.

God, I trust in Your sustaining love and believe that just as You gave me the grace and desire to offer this, so You will also bestow abundant grace to fulfill it.

Information on resources to aid in preparation for taking the vow of nonviolence and copies of the vow in triplicate form can be obtained from the Pax Christi USA national office.

About the Author

Mary Lou Kownacki, OSB, is executive director of Alliance for International Monasticism (AIM), communications director of the Benedictine Sisters of Erie, Pa., and executive director of the Inner City Art House in Erie. She served as national coordinator of Pax Christi USA from 1986 to 1991. Sister Mary Lou has written extensively on the spirituality of nonviolence, published a book on the relationship between monasticism and the peace movement, a book of poetry, a book of prayers for the millennium and other prayers, stories and articles published by magazines, publishers and organizations.

About the Artist

Helen David Brancato, IHM, is an internationally recognized artist from Philadelphia, Pa. She is the director of the Southwest Community Enrichment Art Center. Sister Helen David draws inspiration for her art from the poor, focusing on issues such as homelessness, peace, and those who work for the oppressed. She is a frequent contributor to Pax Christi publications and *Witness Magazine*.